Animals

Illustrated by René Mettler
Written by Gallimard Jeunesse
and René Mettler

A FIRST DISCOVERY BOOK

SCHOLASTIC INC.   Cartwheel
                   ·B·O·O·K·S·®
New York   Toronto   London   Auckland   Sydney
Mexico City   New Delhi   Hong Kong   Buenos Aires

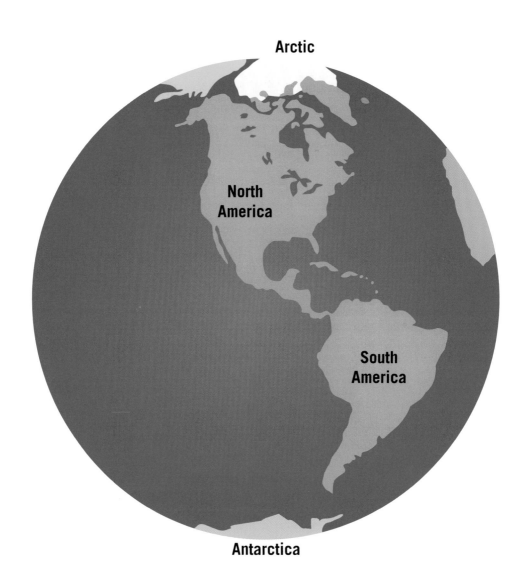

Arctic

North
America

South
America

Antarctica

Turn the page

live on each continent.

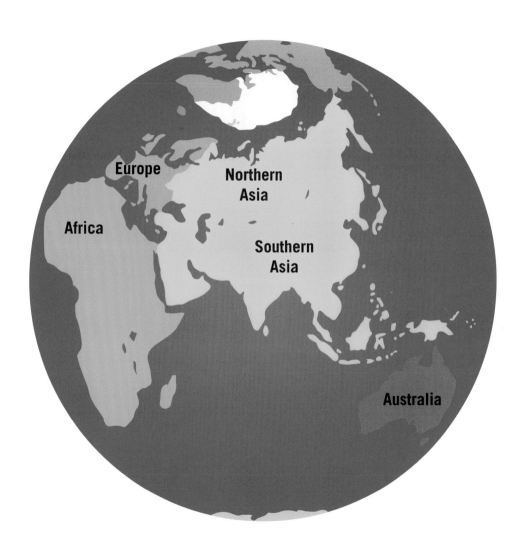

to discover all kinds of animals!

In North America...

The bald eagle is the symbol of the United States. It can be found from Alaska to Florida.

The striped skunk lives in forests and suburbs from southern Canada to northern Mexico.

The raccoon washes its food before eating it.

The bison weighs almost a ton. It eats many pounds of food each day.

The skunk leans on its front paws
and sprays a smelly liquid
at its predators.

This eagle is 31½ inches long
and has a 7-foot wingspan.

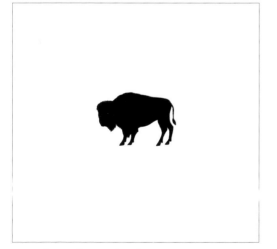

American Indians used the
skin of the bison to make
teepees and clothing.

In April or May,
this mammal gives birth
to 4 or 5 babies.

In South America . . .

The condor lives in the Andes Mountains at more than 10,000 feet above sea level.

The toco toucan makes its nest in trees in tropical rain forests from Guyana to Argentina.

The llama lives in treeless plains, called steppes, and semidesert regions, especially in Peru.

The giant anteater lives in tropical areas and eats termites.

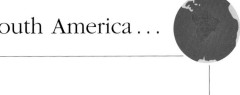

When the toucan sleeps with
its beak and tail on its back,
it is a ball of feathers.

This is the biggest bird of
prey in the world.
It can spot food from far away.

This mammal uses its
long, sticky tongue to
catch insects.

The llama can carry a
heavy load 16 miles a day
on mountain paths.

The anaconda is about 20 to 26 feet long. It stays still for several days at a time as it digests.

The common marmoset lives in the forest. It makes a chattering sound when it talks.

When the sloth hangs upside down from a branch, it turns its head around to stay upright.

The tiny hummingbird hovers next to a flower and uses its long beak to drink the nectar.

The saiga antelope lives in the plains and deserts. Its big nose helps it breathe in the dusty air.

The bactrian camel can go for 12 days without water. It can carry cargo.

The wolf still lives in packs in northern Asia and eats mostly mammals.

The red-breasted goose breeds in Arctic Siberia. It is a rare bird.

The female great hornbill
lays her eggs in a hole in a tree.
Her mate brings her food.

The babirusa lives on the
shores of rivers and lakes.
It eats fruits, nuts, and insects.

The cobra is used by
snake charmers.
But the cobra is really deaf.

The walking stick insect
can hide easily because
it looks like a branch.

The tiger eats antelopes, deer, wild boar, and fish. It can leap more than 15 feet!

The rhinoceros weighs 1 to 3 tons and eats leaves and branches.

The giant panda lives in China and eats 20 to 40 pounds of food a day.

The orangutan lives in the trees of rain forests. It eats fruit, honey, and insects.

In Europe...

The ladybug lays its eggs
on the underside of leaves
and eats hundreds of aphids.

The barn swallow lives in Europe
from April to August. Then it
travels to Africa for the winter.

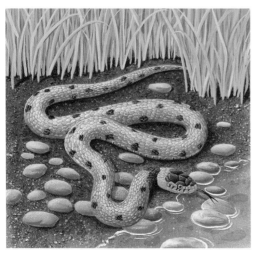

The ringed snake is a very good
swimmer and likes freshwater.
It is not a poisonous snake.

The female common mallard duck
uses her feathers to make her nest.
But the feathers grow back.

The marmot lives in the mountains. It hibernates from October to May.

The badger lives in a sett — a group of tunnels underground. It hunts at night.

The fox lives in forests and prairies. It sleeps in a den.

In autumn, the squirrel buries nuts in different spots for the winter.

The red kangaroo lives in central Australia. Her young, called a joey, stays in her pouch for nine months.

The duck-billed platypus is a mammal. But it has a beak like a duck and lays eggs.

A koala eats mostly eucalyptus lea- ves. It rests for about 20 hours a day.

The sulfur-crested cockatoo lives in the forest. It eats seeds, fruits, nuts, and insects.

The angelfish swims
among the coral reefs.

The great white shark has sharp
teeth. It is the most dangerous
animal in the ocean.

The blue whale swims in the
cold waters of the south. It can
weigh as much as 25 elephants!

The octopus has eight arms.
When it's scared, it shoots ink
into the water to hide itself.

In Africa . . .

The crocodile is a large reptile.
It dozes on the riverbank
as it waits for its prey.

The marabou stork builds its nest
in trees near water. It makes
noise by rattling its bill.

The zebra lives on the plains
with giraffes, gnus, and kudus.

The okapi was not discovered
until 1901. It is the closest
living relative of the giraffe.

The fennec fox lives in
the desert. It has large ears
that help it stay cool.

The dromedary lives in
the desert. It can go several
days without water.

To hide, the desert horned viper
burrows into the sand. Only its
eyes stay aboveground.

The East African oryx
uses its horns
to defend itself.

The gorilla makes its nest
in the rain forests,
mainly along the equator.

The savannah elephant eats bark,
fruit, grass, and leaves. It can drink
up to 50 gallons of water a day.

The hippopotamus stays in
the water during the day
and eats at night.

The lion lives on the open plains
of Africa. It eats gnus, antelopes,
giraffes, and other animals.

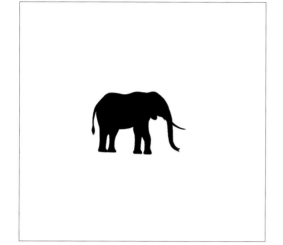

This gigantic plant-eating mammal has huge ears that help keep the animal cool.

This animal walks on all fours. But it stands up to attack its enemies and beats its fists on its chest.

The lion lives in a group called a pride. At night, the lionesses hunt for food.

This animal eats up to 120 pounds of food each day and weighs between 3,000 and 7,000 pounds!

In the Arctic...

The Arctic tern migrates from the Arctic to Antarctica in winter, a 12,000-mile journey round-trip.

When it's very cold, the polar bear will dig a den in the snow and curl up inside.

The musk ox eats plants that grow on the tundra in the north of Canada, Alaska, and Greenland.

The harp seal gives birth between January and April. The pup has white fur.

In Antarctica...

The emperor penguin keeps his egg warm by balancing it on his feet under his stomach.

This large bird eats fish and insects. It usually lays two eggs in May or June.

The Weddell seal swims under the ice. It finds a hole so it can breathe.

The macaroni penguin lays two eggs. The parents take turns caring for the eggs.

Learn fun facts
about these animals!

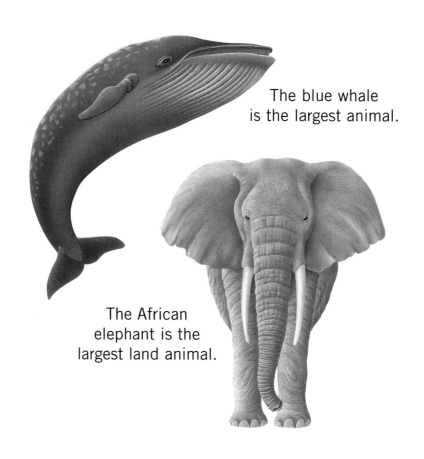

The blue whale is the largest animal.

The African elephant is the largest land animal.

The emperor penguin
raises its young
in the coldest
temperatures
in the world.

The hummingbird
is the tiniest bird.

The panda
is one of the
rarest animals
in the world.